HAPPILY WEALTHY

HAPPINESS, SUCCESS, RICH AND WEALTHY

SHREYA MAITHANI

Made with ❤ on the Notion Press Platform
www.notionpress.com

Dedicated

to every person who has a strong will to achieve their dreams.

Contents

Foreword

A very warm hello to my dear readers.

I am Shreya Maithani an Economics Hons. Student having a keen interest in finance related matters. According to indiatimes.com, the 20s is the most difficult age in life. It's the phase where so many things change in our lives and it all happens so fast. There angst, discovery, unpredictability and a sense of self realisation. It's the time when we truly leave childhood behind and enter a whole new world of responsibility. At this age it is very important to go on with a clear mindset towards a set goal. But how to a set goal, how to make enough money to satisfy all your needs and luxuries, how to be happy and satisfied, etc. questions like this are going to be answered further. If I summarise this whole book in 1 sentence then it will go like; 'happiness and money both has to be in growth with age and time.' Wonder how? Then read this interesting piece of work.

Happy reading!
Shreya Maithani

Preface

I have written this book for everyone who's struggling to find their place in the world, struggling daily for money, and also for those who have money but struggling for mental peace and happiness.

Acknowledgements

This endeavor would not have been possible without my parents, teachers, and friends who made me worthy enough to write a motivational book.

Content

Prologue

Hi I am going to tell you some ways to not only live your life but enjoy it being happy , healthy and wealthy.

Before you start reading,

- Sit in a quiet, clean and warm place.
- Make sure you are comfortable because this will help you to focus more.
- Remove distractions like cell phones, tabs, speakers etc.
- Drink plenty of water.

~

"
"Whatever the mind can conceive and believe, it can achieve."

\- NAPOLEON HILL

"Those who don't manage their money will always work for those who do"

\- DAVE RAMSEY
"

CHAPTER ONE

CAN MONEY BUY HAPPINESS?

According to global wealth distribution 2020, we have only 1 % of millionaires (having income more than US$1million), 11% of middle class (having income of US$100k to 1 million), poor (US$10k to 100k) and miserable (US$10k).

46% of the world's wealth share is in the hands of millionaires, 39% is with middle class, 14% is with poor and 1% is with miserable.

The catastrophe of this precious data given is that, 1% of the total world's adult population itself holds 46% of the world's wealth share. They help in growing the economy as entrepreneurs and billionaires often reinvest their wealth, weather in the company or the stock market. These huge quantities of wealth are used to expand their business and thus, provide services at a more efficient and likely cheaper rate. Thus the economy grows for all.

Ummm.... so are you wandering about why I am talking about this data and the contribution made by riches in our economy?

The simple answer to this is that, if you want to be rich and wealthy and successful in life, first thing you must do is respect rich and successful people and their works.

According to a survey 82% of the wealthy people were happy, while 98% of the poor were unhappy. As here we are talking about money and happiness together, so a big question arises that:

"CAN MONEY BUY YOU HAPPINESS"

Research says :

- Money helps people avoid many of the day-to-day hassles that cause stress,
- The researchers surveyed more than 450000 people to look for a correlation between each person's emotional wellbeing and their level of income. The researchers found that money does increase one's emotional wellbeing , but only up to a certain point.
- In a six month experiment , people who received cash transfers of $10000 generally reported feeling happier than people who did not receive the payment.

According to these sentences it is sure that money can buy happiness, but it is temporary and limited.

> "*happiness is not in the mere possession of money; it lies in the joy of achievement, in the thrill of crreative effort.*
> *- Franklin D. Roosevelt*"

Millionaire are happy, but not extremely happy.

But the results showed that millionaires were around 8 out of 10 on their self-reported happiness. On an average the rich were significantly more satisfied with their lives than anyone else. The researchers were also able to show that active leisure activities were directly related to life satisfaction. The more active someone was, the better they were doing with their life and vice versa.

"you aren't wealthy until you have something money can't buy.
- Garth Brooks"

CHAPTER TWO

WHY PEOPLE REMAIN POOR?

There are 2 broad views to why people stay poor:

Everyone has dreams but not everyone possesses the power, knowlede, ability, talent or motivation to make their dreams a reality.

Other, the poverty trap view, differences in opportunities which stem access to wealth.

But as we know, nothing is impossible; you'll be able to achieve anything if you change your daily silly habits. All successful people possess certain truths and habits, principles that make them the success that they are.

Now, I 'am going to share with you an amazing survey/study conducted by Thomas.C.Corley interviewed 128 Americans who make $35000 or less in gross annual income and have $5000 or less in liquid assets. The research exhibit that wealthy people undeniably have what Corley calls, "rich habits"

Among them are they don't watch more than 1 hr of TV daily, They count calories and they floss their teeth. You might not see the connection between good oral hygiene and a healthy bank account but flowering tasks discipline, if you don't have that, it's easy to fall into what Corley said "poverty habits"

Here are seven poverty habits that handcuff people to a life of low income.

- **Poor people do not have a plan and a set goal** – "95 % of the poor people in my study had no life plan" Corley wrote. "without a blue print, without long term goal, we are like leaves on a fall day, floating in the air aimlessly"

While rich people list, what they want to achieve daily, weekly, monthly and they can tell you where they want to be in 20 years. Poor people just sort of wing it.

Hence, you don't have to be rich to make a plan, you do need a plan if you want to be rich.

- **They overspend** – many studies says that saving is the best path to be rich. Saving your money and then investing it, it's like planting an acorn and watching it sprout into a tree. But poor people always overspend their money in unnecessary things.

If you barely make enough money to pay your bills and can't save, obvious solution is to make more money. That leads to the next poverty habit.

- **They only have 1 stream of income** – poor people spend their whole life working on a single earning source and whole family is dependent on a single earner.

A 2019 US census bureau a study found that only 8.8% women and 8.0% of men have 2 or more jobs.

Corley found that 65% of wealthy people had at least 3 different streams of income set up prior to making their first $1 million.

- **They never read and educate themselves** – poor people believe reading non fictional books a waste of time. But reading is must in every individual's life.

Wealthy people not only work dual jobs, they make time to read too. But they are not reading novels or Stephen king stories.

They read educational and self improvement books. Corley found that only 8% of the low earnerners read educational or self-improvement books.

"Success requires growth, he wrote; that growth comes from reading and educating yourself on a daily basis"

- **They get into toxic relationships** – psychology does play an important role in being rich. You must have a cant do attitude but it's hard to maintain one of you, associate with can't do people. Corley found that only 4% of how income people associate with "success minded people"

Corley wrote,
"You are only going to succeed in life if you surround yourself with the right type of people."
That is to say people who are encouraging, positive, curious, and helpful.

- **They engage in negative self talk** – unsuccessful people waste half of their life with a negative kind of thoughts crawling in their minds. These negative thoughts cover their creative and positive side of brain completely.

Corley wrote, "When you allow negativity to rule your thoughts you are programming your brain for failure,

"You'll have no chance in life at breaking out of your current financial or life circumstances; there negative thoughts will become beliefs that act like computer programs."

At end,

Corley wrote, "Adopting one rich habit has the effect of eliminating many poor habits"

so stop watching so much TV, read more, start making plans, think positive and find extra income streams.

> *"Five major causes of failure: drifting without aim or purpose, lack of self-discipline, a negative mental attitude, no ambition above mediocrity, lack of persistence in carrying out what you started.*
>
> *- Napoleon Hill"*

CHAPTER THREE

RICH OR WEALTHY

We all are in the same race to get success in every path we take. But did you actually know what success is,

According to dictionary Cambridge,

"Success is the fact that you have achieved what you want; doing well and becoming famous, rich, wealthy etc".

WAIT!

Here I have mentioned RICH and WEALTHY two different terms.

Do you know the difference between rich and wealthy?

Many people think that being rich and wealthy are same thing.

But there is a difference between the two: the rich have lots of money nut the wealthy don't worry about money.

How many days could you survive if you stopped working today?

How long could you survive on the amount of money you have?

Wealthy is a person's ability to survive X number of days forward.

RICH works for their money, they buys expensive cars and clothes, and lives a flashy lifestyle. On the other hand a wealthy person make passive income from assets buys real estates and stocks and lives below their means.

"the real measure of our wealth is how much wealth be worth if we lost all our money"............John Henry Jowett

It's all your pick, weather you want to be rich or wealthy or you can be both too. But whatever you will be, be happy and grateful for what you have.

It will be little difficult to set a goal or to decide what you actually want to be. Our next topic is related to this problem.

CHAPTER FOUR

SET A GOAL

The path towards our goals may not always run smoothly or be easy, but having goals, weather big or small is part of what makes life good, it gives us a sense of meaning and purpose, points us in the direction we want to go and gets us interested and engaged, all which are good for our overall happiness.

Where to start-

- Selection- list out various jobs and career according to your field and interest. Analyse each of them taking salary, work, or the things you want to see in your dream career into consideration. Once you have done with all this, compare them, and select one. It doesn't matter what, as long as its something you want to do- ideally something you are interested in or feel excited by.

- Write It down- writing down our goals increases our chances of sticking with them. Write down how you will know you have reached your goals and when you would like to have achieved it by. Write your goals in terms of what you want not what you don't want. For example, "I want to be able to wear my favourite jeans again", rather

than "I don't want to be overweight anymore"
- Breakdown your goal- having several smaller goals make each of them a bit easier and gives us a feeling of success along the way, which also makes it more likely that will stay on track towards our bigger goal.
- Plan your first step
- Keep going
- Celebrate

Always remember one thing that while setting goals, they must answer the highly specific questions of who, what, where, when and why.

CHAPTER FIVE

HAPPILY WEALTHY

Question yourself,

What are the things which make you feel sad or stressed?

Do you appreciate what you already have?

If not then this might be a reason for your sad and stressed out days.

First thing you must follow is to appreciate what you already have. If you sit around thinking , " I don't like my house , I wish I had a better one" or "I can't wait to got a new car because I am embarrassed to drive this one" , you are sending out negative vibrations with thoughts . According to the law of attraction negative, slow-moving thoughts will not create anything positive. Instead, you need to love your house or your car. Or simply be grateful that you have a roof over your head, a bed to sleep in, or food on your table. The more you give appreciation to what you already have, the more likely it will be that you will be able to acquire more.

These days being rich and wealthy might be easy but being happy is a tough task.

Here are few simple steps which I suggest you to follow until it become a habit.

- **Waking up at 5 a.m.**

Waking up early means you are already ahead of everyone else. Waking up earlier gives you more time to-
-workout
-plan your day
-work on business
-be more productive
It's a huge life hack which gives you more time to achieve your goals.

According to Ayurveda, the early hours between 4 a.m. and 5 a.m. are dominated by the VATA DOSHA, the biological energy which is ruled by space and air. The vata dosha governs mental activities, activities and body movements. When you rise at this early hour, take advantage of this added time in your day to get out of bed and move and think.

> *"Rich people don't sleep 8 hrs a day, that's the 3rd of your life, it isn't for 24 hrs in a day. You cannot sleep 8 hrs a day. You can't live in LA and wakeup at 8 o clock in the morning. Its 11 o clock in the east coast and the stock market being open for 2 hrs. They already making decisions and you were sleeping. The bible says, he who loves to sleep and the folding of hands, poverty will sat upon you like a thief at the night."*
> *-Steve haverly*

- **Writing down your thoughts before bed.**

Writing before bed will improve your quality of sleep. Here's what you can write down:-

-your goals for tomorrow

-what you have grateful for

-any negative thoughts.

This will improve your mental health dramatically. Writing improves your memory, builds vocabulary and refines your communication skills. Not to forget that writing can be very relaxing, especially if you lead a busy and stressful life.

To build a writing habit, you must build a reading habit.

- **Read 20 pages a day**

Reading will strengthen your mind and also-

-increase your focus

-increase your knowledge

-increase your self confidence

Just 20 pages a day will give you a huge return in life.

Do you know that successful people share a common habit that makes them successful. Almost every successful person read, they read a lot, because they see books as a gateway to knowledge.

- **Learning an online skill 30 minutes a day**

Your mind is racing with hundreds of thoughts every minute.

Take 10 minutes to-

-sit in silence

-practice mindfulness

-give your mind a break

-be present in the moment

This is an underrated habit for your mental health.
Sitting in silence may help your health in several ways-
-lowering blood pressure
-improving concentration and focus
-calming racing thoughts
-stimulating brain growth
Each one of us is aware of the rhyme, 'EARLY TO BED, EARLY TO RISE, MAKES A MAN HEALTHY WEALTHY AND WISE'
We have already talked about waking up , now about sleep.

- **Create a proper sleep schedule.**

Sleep is essential for your performance, mental health , reducing stress, improving your mood.
You can do this for deep and quality sleep-
-no screen 2 hours before bed.
-no eating 2 hours before bed
-make your room cooler
-use blackout curtains.
Adding to all these, I am suggesting you to medicate daily for at least 10 to 15 minutes , take a walk in nature every day, and you add some more points according to your lifestyle.
World's happiest person, 'Mathieu Richard' 69 years old Tibetan Buddhist monk originally from France. He says that the secret to being happy takes just 15 minutes a day. Yes, you heard it right!
If you meditate just only for 15 minutes a day, you'll feel increase in your ability to focus. Meditation helps increase your focus and attention.

CHAPTER SIX

TYCOON

Now, if we talk about being RICH and WEALTHY, I will suggest you some books –

-think and grow rich by NAPOLEON HILL

-how rich people think by STEVE SIEBOLD

-the richest man in Babylon by GEORGE SAMUEL

Reading does play a catalytic role in your journey to become rich . a majority of successful and rich people share reading as a common trait.

But generally speaking , you can't become rich just by reading books.

Self made wealthy people don't become rich by accident. Instead, they often take intentional actions to make money and build wealth.

To be successful in life you must-

Identify your goals

-Before you get started on becoming rich , device a financial plan. Here are a few questions you may ask yourself as you put your plan together.

- What does being rich mean?
- Is there a particular net worth I'd like to hit?
- What is my monthly budget goal?

- Am I looking to put money aside to invest or to pay off debt?
- Am I looking to achieve early retirement?

Get specific with your answers so you know your exact goal. Once you have your big-picture vision established, break it down into smaller short term goals that are easier to achieve. By creating this roadmap, you should have clearer sense of what your destination is and how to get there.

You don't need a six figure job or family money to become a millionaire. Instead, you need to –

- Start early savings
- Avoid unnecessary spending
- Save 20% of your income
- You must have 2 source of income

Once you get money learn how to manage money.

CHAPTER SEVEN

MANAGE YOUR MONEY

Now let us discuss about managing your money.

Do you know saving money is a step towards making money. So start budgeting and saving your money. Without money management; personal finances are a bit of mystery. This can lead to over spending and living pay check to pay check. Money management can help you have a better handle on your income and spending so you can make decisions that improve your financial status. It is important to learn how to manage your money.

Here are some ways to manage your money better, suggested by the renowned website 'the balance'

1. **Have a budget** – many people don't budget because they don't want to go through what they think will be a boring process of listing your expenses, adding up numbers , and making sure everything lines up. If you are bad with money, you don't have room for excuses with budgeting. If all it takes to get your spending on track is a few hours working a budget each month, why wouldn't you do it? Instead of focusing on the process of

creating a budget, focus on the value that budgeting will bring to your life.

2. **Use the budget**- your budget is useless if you make it then it collect dust in a folder tucked away in your bookshelf or file cabinet. Refer to it often throughout the month to month to help guide your spending decisions. Update it as you pay bills and spend on other monthly expenses. At any given time during the month, you should have an idea of how much money you're able to spend, considering any expenses you have left to pay.

3. **Make sure you're paying the best prices** – you can make the most of our money comparison shopping, ensuring that you're paying the lowest prises for the products and services. Look for discounts, coupons and cheaper alternatives whenever you can.

4. **Limit your credit card purchases**.

5. **Contribute to savings regularly**

Looking beyond these being rich comes with struggles only the rich can relate with. And some of those are under listed-

- There is never enough time
- They are not seen for who they really are
- They don't raise their family the regular way
- They find it more difficult to spend money than make it
- They struggle to find a balance in their lives
- They are under stiff pressure
- They battle with their desires
- They are obsessed with their passions
- They find it difficult to understand who is realistic with them

As you know that money can buy you a clock but not time. The money we got right after birth is time. Time is the first money you hold, no one can steal it from you. So spend it wisely. I'm pretty sure that it will give you good return in future. So to save your time you must build a timetable, taking all these things into consideration that I've mentioned in above paragraphs. Make a proper schedule reduces chaos and wastage of time, because half of the time we waste only in thinking what to do now or next.

Money can easily buy you **food, a clock, a home, education, make-up or meditation**; however it can't buy **nutrition, a home, knowledge, beauty or health.**

CHAPTER EIGHT

RICH OF THE RICHEST

RICHEST PERSON IN THE WORLD

1. *Bernard Arnault and family – CEO of Hennessey Lous Vuitton – net worth $180 billion*
2. *Elon Musk – CEO of Tesla – net worth $139 billion*
3. *Gautam Adani – CEO of Adani roup – net worth $124 billion*

HAPPIEST BILLIONARE IN THE WORLD
Herbert Wertheim – an inventor- net worth 4 billion dollar
RICHEST WOMEN IN THE WORLD
Françoise Bettencourt Meyers
YOUNGEST SELF MADE BILLIONARE
Alexander Wang (25) – CEO of scale AI
YOUNGEST BILLIONARE IN THE WORLD
Divya Gokulnath (36) – CEO of Byju's
Nikhil Kamath (35) – CEO of Zerodha
YOUNGEST BILLIONARE IN INDIA
United States of America

HENCE,

Key to be rich – savings, investment, time management and lot of hardwork.